Wandering in th

May Jesus walk beside you in any wilderness you know this Lent

My Goals For Lent

Prayer For Lent

Thank you loving God for the gift of this season of Lent. Thank you for knowing my heart and my need for rhythms in my life. For drawing me into a closer relationship with you throughout the coming days of Lent.

Lord, I read on Ash Wednesday that all come from dust, and to dust all return (Ecclesiastes 3:20).

May I remember the gift of salvation in this season.

May these weeks leading up to Good Friday and the glory of Resurrection Sunday remind me of who you are and how you love me.

May I walk through this season intentionally, please remove distractions that take my gaze away from your glory.

May I quiet the noise that pulls me from you and draws my attention on lesser things.

May I be at peace, may I surrender what has been burdensome, may I repent and turn back to you.

May I see your goodness and your glory in new ways throughout this season of Lent.

May I know the depths of your love for me more fully.

May I feel the pain you endured for my sake.

Draw me closer to you, that I might know you better and understand you more completely. I pray that Lent, for me, is not just about giving things up or taking things on, but that I would give you glory through Lent, Lord. May my actions reflect You, and may I worship You through all that I say and do throughout the weeks to come.

May my praise never cease in this season.

May my worship be unending.

May this season of Lent bring new hope and new healing.

Keeping Track

The journey begins

Lent invites us to consider the time that Jesus spent in the desert and to ponder on our own desert experience. The experience of the desert is necessary to enable us truly to put all our hope in God.

Throughout Christian history, people have found themselves in the desert. Sometimes literally so, as in the case of the Jews who wandered there for forty years. Later, like those who preceded him, and like all of us who follow him, Christ honed his humanity in the desert in obedience to his Father. And he was led there by the Holy Spirit in order to do so. Nothing the devil was able to do could come between Jesus and his Father's will.

We all experience a spiritual desert from time to time when trying to follow Christ. We are offered through the Lenten liturgy an opportunity to strengthen there, with Christ, our own obedience to the Father.

The desert is the place where God can fashion us. We will find God there. By allowing the Spirit to lead us into the desert, as Jesus did, we are strengthened against all adversity, just as Christ was fortified to withstand his later agony in the garden, his passion and death, and so come to the glory of his resurrection.

For all of us, the desert comes in many disguises such as misunderstandings, hurts, violence, depression, rejection or sickness. Ultimately, the desert is telling us, in the only language that really gets home, that we need a look again at our relationship with God. Break away the barriers that separate us from his grace and love. Establish a new beginning and feel the light of the Lord's acceptance on our face and in our hearts. This will allow us to live our best life.

The desert will bloom for all who allow themselves to be led by the Spirit, as Christ was, into whatever form that desert may take. For "these sufferings bring patience . . . patience brings perseverance, and perseverance brings hope. And this hope is not deceptive, because the love of God has been poured into our hearts by the Holy Spirit who has been given to us" Rom, 5:3-4

God is there, waiting for us in the desert. To turn to him is what is meant by 'repentance'. The sufferings of this life, far from driving us away from God, are there to turn us towards him – by finding him in that desert where we are alone with him, where, like Christ in the desert, we find ourselves in tune with God.

Repentance – turning back, is what the desert experience is about. It is why the Lenten liturgy is so important. It seems doubtful that repentance is possible until the 'desert' has convinced us that left to ourselves, we cannot find fulfilment: and in that realisation, the peace of Christ is born within us to transform us and change our daily living.

The Wilderness Experience

In the wilderness experience we can learn and understand about God and His methods and about ourselves. God wants us to have a close relationship with Him.

To walk in the wilderness is to be willing to have our lives stripped back; to go without; to slow down; to empty ourselves in order that God might work in us. Sometimes circumstances do the stripping back for us and sometimes we do it ourselves by choosing disciplines like simplicity.

Turning Back

This Lent is an opportunity for us to reassess our relationship with God and, by pulling out all those barriers that block our closeness with God, we can ask for forgiveness and turn back to God to fully align ourselves with him, to move on after Lent into freedom and peace.

By examining ourselves and turning back we can remove from our lives those obstacles that hurt us and hold us. Take a moment now to think about Lent and write down your goals for Lent.

What can we learn from our own wilderness experience?

'He ate nothing during those days, and at the end of them he was hungry. The devil said to him, "If you are the Son of God, tell this stone to become bread." Jesus answered, "It is written: 'Man shall not live on bread alone.'"' (Luke 4:2-4)

God is our provider. We get a taste of that truth in the times of plenty, when every need is met with abundance and every prayer is answered. It's in our wilderness we truly learn that God is enough.

Pray

Most merciful God, Father of our Lord Jesus Christ, I confess that I have sinned in thought, word and deed. I have not loved you with my whole heart, and mind, and strength. I have not loved my neighbours as myself. I have not forgiven others, as I have been forgiven.

Lord, have mercy.

I have not listened to your call to serve as Christ served me. I have not been true to the mind of Christ. I have grieved your Holy Spirit.

Lord, have mercy.

I confess to you, Eternal God … all my past unfaithfulness: the pride, hypocrisy and impatience of my life.

Lord, have mercy.

My self-indulgent appetites and ways, and my exploitation of other people.

Lord, have mercy.

My anger at my own frustration and my envy of those more fortunate than myself.

Lord, have mercy.

My intemperate love of worldly goods and comforts, and my dishonesty in daily life and work.

Lord, have mercy.

My negligence in prayer and worship, and my failure to commend the faith that is in me.

Lord, have mercy.

Accept my repentance, God of grace, for the wrongs I have done, for my indifference to human need and suffering, to injustice and cruelty.

Accept my repentance, gracious God, for all false judgements, for uncharitable thoughts towards my neighbours and for my prejudice and contempt towards those who differ from me.

Accept my repentance, gracious God, for my waste and pollution of creation and my lack of concern for those who come after me.

Accept my repentance, gracious God. Restore me, good Lord, and let your anger depart from me. Favourably hear me, for your mercy is great. Accomplish in me the work of your salvation, that I may show your glory in the world.

I have not loved you with my whole heart. I have not loved my neighbours as myself. In your mercy forgive what I have been, help me to amend what I am, and direct what I shall be; that I may do justly, love mercy, and walk humbly with you, my God.

Amen.

Throughout this book you will find a prayer for each day of Lent. If time permits nothing else, say these prayers each day of Lent. As you pray notice what stirs in you. Record your feelings and personal prayers. At the end of Lent, look back over your reflections and decide what God has told you about yourself and how you are living your life.

Lent Reflections

Jesus Is Tested in the Wilderness

Luke 4 1-13

Jesus, full of the Holy Spirit, left the Jordan and was led by the Spirit into the wilderness,

2 where for forty days he was tempted by the devil. He ate nothing during those days, and at the end of them he was hungry.

3 The devil said to him, "If you are the Son of God, tell this stone to become bread."

4 Jesus answered, "It is written; 'Man shall not live on bread alone.'"

5 The devil led him up to a high place and showed him in an instant all the kingdoms of the world. 6 And he said to him, "I will give you all their authority and splendour; it has been given to me, and I can give it to anyone I want to. 7 If you worship me, it will all be yours."

8 Jesus answered, "It is written; 'Worship the Lord your God and serve him only.'"

9 The devil led him to Jerusalem and had him stand on the highest point of the temple. "If you are the Son of God," he said, "throw yourself down from here.

10 For it is written; 'He will command his angels concerning you to guard you carefully;

11 they will lift you up in their hands, so that you will not strike your foot against a stone.'"

12 Jesus answered, "It is said: 'Do not put the Lord your God to the test.'"

13 When the devil had finished all this tempting, he left him until an opportune time.

Sunday before Ash Wednesday

Our journey through Lent – Packing

The best journeys deserve good preparation. Let us reflect on how we might prepare for our own Lent journey.

We begin our Lent journey in deep gratitude for all that God has done for us over the years of our lives so far. Sit in silence for a few minutes today, allowing your thoughts to roam over the many ways you've experienced the goodness of God. Take delight in remembering all the good things God is for you.

Call to action.

The Israelite prophet Micah said: "What does the Lord require of you? Only to act justly, love mercy and to walk humbly with your God."

A Prayer for Preparation for Lent

Lord, as I enter Lent help me to draw near to you in praise, stripping away all that distracts me from worship.

God of mercy and source of justice, pour on your people such love and compassion so that I cannot remain silent, I cannot tolerate injustice and poverty. As your grace fills my heart this Lent, so may I be stirred into action to demonstrate your love for all the world and for all creatures that live and move on this earth.

As Jesus resisted temptation by the devil in the wilderness, help me reflect on his faithfulness to You, loving God, his rejection of worldly values and hold these thoughts in my heart throughout Lent and beyond. Lord, may Lent be a time of inward searching that makes me more able to look with compassion at the needs of the world.

Monday before Ash Wednesday

Jesus didn't set foot in the wilderness until he knew who he was. 'You are my Son, whom I love; with you I am well pleased' (Luke 3:22).

Those were the words the Father spoke over him at his baptism, and they must have become even more precious as he trudged through the wilderness.

Meditate on a Bible verse today – one that has meant a lot to you in the past. Carry it around in your mind (and even in your pocket), calling it to mind in each situation you face.

Pray

Forgive me Lord for my apathy, for my lack of courage to speak out. Forgive me when I walk past and don't offer help. Forgive me when I get it wrong. I confess that I am afraid - I don't want to overcome my hidden doubts and prejudices in order to be alongside those who are different from me. I am comfortable in the person I am and don't want to change. I ask that you would lead me into action; give me strength to be a voice crying for justice and peace. Help me to step into another person's shoes, peel off my preconceptions and assumptions, and tread in their footprints. May I be a liberating presence during this Lent and offer love, compassion and whatever is needed to act justly, love mercy and walk humbly with my God.

Shrove Tuesday

An increasing number of studies, especially during the enforced isolation of the pandemic, tell us happiness and wellbeing are found not in isolated individuality but in social connection. It is through strong relationships with family, friends and community that we truly flourish. Wellbeing depends on factors such as a rich sense of community and giving to others. In other words, focusing upon myself is the wrong place to look.

Luke chose this moment in Jesus' story to tell us his family line (Luke 3:23-37). It's as though he imagined Jesus stepping out into uncharted territory, consoled and inspired by the earthly family God had placed him in.

Connect with some of your family today – whether blood relations or 'chosen family'. As you pray for them, send each a message thanking them for the blessings they've brought into your life.

A Prayer for Shrove Tuesday

On this Shrove Tuesday, Lord help me to enjoy and give thanks to you for the bounty you provide for me and remind me to share your gifts with others. As Lent begins tomorrow, prepare my heart and mind to reflect upon the temptation of Jesus for 40 days and nights during his desert experience and what that means for me.

Ash Wednesday

Today is Ash Wednesday, the day we receive ashes on our forehead in the shape of a cross. The ashes are a symbol of our human mortality, expressing the fact that we will die and our only survival is through Christ. When the ashes are put on our forehead in the sign of the cross these words are spoken – "Remember you are dust and to dust you shall return." This is a reminder that we must die and that we live only due to the will of God. God created us from dust. Although our bodies will return to dust, we will live again, thanks to Christ's sacrifice, hence the sign of the cross.

Today is a day of repentance, prayer and fasting. After receiving our ashes, we should pray and meditate on this simple truth; Our bodies come from dust, and to dust they shall return, but our souls will live forever thanks to the sacrifice of Jesus Christ on the cross. The mark of the cross is the sign of forgiveness and healing, connecting us with the presence of God who is before and after, alpha and omega, in time and eternity.

One of the optional phrases in the application of the ashes done in churches today on Ash Wednesday is, "Repent and believe in the Gospel". The word we translate as 'repent' – metanoia – means 'change of heart' or to live life with your belief in the Gospel at its centre. For Christians the person of Jesus Christ is central to the Good News of the Gospel.

Pray

Lord, give me a quiet, humble heart and a clean soul so I will be ready to listen to your word.

Action

Spend time today in prayer and contemplation.

The Collect (Prayer for the Day) Almighty and everlasting God, you hate nothing that you have made and forgive the sins of all those who are penitent. Create and make in us new and contrite hearts, that we, worthily lamenting our sins and acknowledging our wretchedness, may receive from you, the God of all mercy, perfect remission and forgiveness; through Jesus Christ our Redeemer. Amen.

Isaiah 58.1-12

Shout out, do not hold back! Lift up your voice like a trumpet! Announce to my people their rebellion, to the house of Jacob their sins. Yet day after day they seek me and delight to know my ways, as if they were a nation that practised righteousness and did not forsake the ordinance of their God; they ask of me righteous judgements, they delight to draw near to God. 'Why do we fast, but you do not see? Why humble ourselves, but you do not notice?' Look, you serve your own interest on your fast-day, and oppress all your workers. Look, you fast only to quarrel and to fight and to strike with a wicked fist. Such fasting as you do today will not make your voice heard on high.

Is such the fast that I choose, a day to humble oneself? Is it to bow down the head like a bulrush, and to lie in sackcloth and ashes? Will you call this a fast, a day acceptable to the Lord? Is not this the fast that I choose: to loose the bonds of injustice, to undo the thongs of the yoke, to let the oppressed go free, and to break every yoke? Is it not to share your bread with the hungry, and bring the homeless poor into your house; when you see the naked, to cover them, and not to hide yourself from your own kin? Then your light shall break forth like the dawn, and your healing shall spring up quickly; your vindicator shall go before you, the glory of the LORD shall be your rear guard.

Then you shall call, and the Lord will answer; you shall cry for help, and he will say, Here I am. If you remove the yoke from among you, the pointing of the finger, the speaking of evil, if you offer your food to the hungry and satisfy the needs of the afflicted, then your light shall rise in the darkness and your gloom be like the noonday. The Lord will guide you continually, and satisfy your needs in parched places, and make your bones strong; and you shall be like a watered garden, like a spring of water, whose waters never fail. Your ancient ruins shall be rebuilt; you shall raise up the foundations of many generations; you shall be called the repairer of the breach, the restorer of streets to live in.

The Imposition of the Ashes

God alone is holy and just and good. Thanks be to God. Christ comes that we might be free from shame. Thanks be to God. The Holy Spirit anoints us with the oil of gladness that calls us to new life. Thanks be to God.

You are invited to make the sign of the cross on your own forehead, with ash or with oil or just by making the sign. As we make the sign of the cross, we pray together; Gracious God, give me courage to know that I am dust and to dust I shall return. Help me to turn away from sin and be faithful to Christ. May I bear the sign of the cross in peace, knowing that it is the tree of life. Amen.

May you be enriched with God's grace and nourished with God's blessing; May God defend you in trouble and keep you from evil; May God accept your prayers, and absolve you from your offences, for the sake of Jesus Christ, our Redeemer. Amen.

Pray

A Prayer for Spiritual Communion inspired by Richard of Chichester (1198- 1253)

Thanks be to you, Christ Jesus, for all the benefits you have given me, for all the pains and insults you have borne for me. I ask you to be present with me spiritually in my heart. O most merciful redeemer, friend and brother, may I know you more clearly, love you more dearly, and follow you more nearly, day by day. Amen.

And now we offer ourselves, all that we have and are, to serve you faithfully in the world, through Jesus Christ our Redeemer, to whom with you and the Holy Spirit be all honour and glory, now and forever. Amen.

Lord, we come to ask your healing, teach us of love; all unspoken shame revealing, teach us of love. Take our selfish thoughts and actions, petty feuds, divisive factions, hear us now to you appealing, teach us of love. Soothe away our pain and sorrow, hold us in love; grace we cannot buy or borrow, hold us in love. Though we see but dark and danger, though we spurn both friend and stranger, though we often dread tomorrow, hold us in love. As our grateful prayers continue, make the faith that we have in you more than just an empty token, fill us with love. Help us live for one another, bind us in love.

Prayer Requests

Thursday after Ash Wednesday

What did Jesus pack for the journey into the desert? There's no way to know, but we can do our own 'packing', before we set out. What have you learnt over recent months? What new gifts have you received? What old blessings have you rediscovered? What do you think God is telling you to hold on to in this season of Lent?

Do some journaling, writing down what you want to achieve through your Lent journey.

We assume Jesus travelled his wilderness journey alone, but it's notable that it began in a public place with lots of onlookers (Luke 3:21).

21 When all the people were being baptised, Jesus was baptised too. And as he was praying, heaven was opened 22 and the Holy Spirit descended on him in bodily form like a dove. And a voice came from heaven: "You are my Son, whom I love; with you I am well pleased."

It's easy to get caught up in our own concerns, but the people around us are on a journey too, and we all need the encouragement of fellow-travellers.

Go for a walk with friends or family. Talk to each other about the journeys you're on and where you'd like to have got to by Easter.

Pray for Others

God of mercy and love, let me serve you in this world. I pray for desert people, who live in a dry, parched land, who lack water, who travel constantly so that they might live. Give them living water. Let the deserts bloom into flower. I pray that those who work on climate change may find solutions so that the erosion of soil may be halted or reversed.

I pray that water and other vital supplies might not be used as a weapon of war in countries where resources are scarce. I pray that we can share vaccines with the whole world so we all might be safe from disease. God of mercy and love let me serve you in our world

People to Pray For

Friday after Ash Wednesday

Setting Out

'Jesus, full of the Holy Spirit, left the Jordan and was led by the Spirit into the wilderness...' (Luke 4:1). This week we think about leaving home, embarking on a new journey and being led to unexpected places.

Pray

I pray for countries where justice seems far away and where human rights are ignored. I pray that tortured prisoners are not forgotten.

I pray that the dignity of life is respected and remember those who have lost that dignity through age or infirmity or neglect.

I pray for situations where the gender of a baby may lead to abandonment, where women are not offered the same opportunities, or are actively demeaned or mutilated.

Please give me the courage and opportunity to act. To challenge injustice and seek to affirm your love for all humankind.

God of mercy and love, let me serve you in our world and show me how to do this.

Saturday after Ash Wednesday

Luke tells us that the Spirit led Jesus into the wilderness (Luke 4:1). Does that mean Jesus set out without knowing where he was going, or did the Spirit overrule his plans? If you're the sort of person who likes to be in control, it can be hard to let the Spirit lead you.

Fast from one of your regular daily activities today – a meal, a TV programme you normally watch or your time on social media. See where the Spirit leads you in the time you free up.

Pray

I pray for those who have no peace – for those who are troubled and torn apart by lack of self-esteem, for those who torment and victimise the vulnerable. I pray for men and women affected by violence in their home and for those who live by violence. May they see the error of their ways and turn to You. I pray for those who are trafficked and for those who organise and profit from selling other humans, may they see the error of their ways and turn to You. May they learn of your love and somehow come to newness of life even in the midst of despair. God of mercy and love, let me serve you in this world.

Loving Lord, let me not stand aside and tolerate lack of basic human resources, dehumanising practices, or the use of violence to disempower your people. Give me strength to act and challenge hatred, and instead bring your justice and mercy. In your name I humbly ask that I may be a channel for your peace and love.

Please Lord show me what your will is.

The Wilderness Experience Can Bring Spiritual Growth

Don't grumble or complain while in a wilderness experience. It's easy to not feel thankful about anything and to grumble about your circumstances when you can't see a way out of it. This is what the Israelites did while in the desert. Consequently, this may have had a detrimental effect on them, although it probably also revealed a lot about the state of their hearts. They ended up wandering around in the wilderness for forty years. It should have only been a relatively short journey.

Complaining and constant grumbling about your situation does not bring glory to God. That said, there is a difference between complaining to God, which can be an act of worship, and complaining about God. The former is offering to him your situation but still trusting in his goodness and ability to see what is best for you. You needn't be afraid to bring your lamentations and disappointments to God in heartfelt prayer. You can tell God how bad you are feeling. He is big enough to handle this. Some of the Psalms are lamentations.

Exodus 17:1-7 tells us that the Israelites complained to Moses about the plans that God had given him for them. They questioned whether God had brought them out of Egypt to die of thirst.

Verse 7 tells us that Moses named the place Massah and Meribah (meaning testing and quarrelling respectively) because the Israelites quarrelled and put God to the test, "Is the Lord among us or not?"

When we complain about God, we are questioning his goodness. This not only demonstrates a lack of faith, but can actually erode our faith.

When you begin to say phrases like "I hate my life" or "I'll never be out of this desert", that colours your own perspective on everything. Soon your words become a self-fulfilling prophecy. You begin to hate every aspect of your life and find that in every aspect you are failing.

Similarly, complaining about God and making pronouncements about him such as, "You never bless me – you always bless someone else", can erode our own relationship with God and our sense of trust in him.

Complaining also rewires your brain so you actually end up feeling worse as you internalise these words. It can become a habit which fills your minds with toxic thoughts that prevents us from receiving His grace and from working in our lives

Be thankful and worship God while in a wilderness experience

When we speak out or make positive affirmations about God, even if we don't fully believe them at the time we are saying them, we can begin to revitalise our faith in him.

First Sunday of LENT

The First Week of Lent

Sunday

Whether he'd planned it or not, the wilderness must have felt like a daunting destination for Jesus, yet Luke tells us he emerged transformed – in the power of the Spirit (Luke 4:14).

Do some journaling today about a time in your life when you found yourself in a place you didn't want to be. How did you get there? What was God's involvement? How were you different afterwards?

Pray

Lord God, you who breathed the spirit of life within me. Draw out of me the light and life you created. Help me to find my way back to you. Help me to use my life to reflect your glory and to serve others as your son Jesus did.

This Lent think about:

Fasting from selfishness and be compassionate to others.

Fasting from anger and be filled with patience.

Fasting from sadness and be filled with gratitude.

Fasting from worries and trust in God.

Fasting from complaining and be positive.

Fasting from pressures and be prayerful.

Fasting from pessimism and be filled with hope.

Fasting from bitterness and forgive yourself and others.

Fasting from grudges and be reconciled.

Fasting from words and be quiet so you can listen.

Fasting from hurting words and be kind.

The First Week of Lent

Monday

Forty days is a long time to be away from home. The Gospels make it clear that Jesus loved people and parties, so he must have missed being with his loved ones. Take time today to connect with someone who is away from home. Ask how they're doing and ask how you can pray for them? Hold them in your prayers today.

Pray

Loving God, you call us back to you. I feel your call for me deep in my heart and I know you want me to turn back as much as I know I need to return.

Please, Lord, give me the wisdom to know how to return.

Make my journey back to you this Lent one of grace, forgiveness and gentle love.

Self Examination During Lent

The Wilderness Experience Can Bring Spiritual Growth

Be thankful and worship God while in a wilderness experience

When we speak out or make positive affirmations about God, even if we don't fully believe them at the time we are saying them, we can begin to revitalise our faith in him.

In Deuteronomy 31:19-21, God tells Moses to write down a song, which is also known as the Song of Moses. This is towards the end of the Israelites wilderness experience. It would be easy for the Israelites to forget what God had done for them and to go back to their former ways. Therefore, this is a song of praise and thanksgiving chronicling God's mighty deeds in leading the Israelites out of captivity and through the desert. It tells of his faithfulness and provision through all the hardship and times of testing.

"Now write down this song and teach it to the Israelites and have them sing it, so that it may be a witness for me against them. When I have brought them into the land flowing with milk and honey, the land I promised on oath to their ancestors, and when they eat their fill and thrive, they will turn to other gods and worship them, rejecting me and breaking my covenant. And when many disasters and calamities come on them, this song will testify against them, because it will not be forgotten by their descendants. I know what they are disposed to do, even before I bring them into the land I promised them on oath.

In Deuteronomy 32: 46-47, Moses adds:

"Take to heart all the words I have solemnly declared to you this day, so that you may command your children to obey carefully all the words of this law. They are not just idle words for you—they are your life. By them you will live long in the land you are crossing the Jordan to possess."

This highlights the importance of worshipping God.

When we are in the desert, we also need to sing of God's deeds. We need to give thanksgiving and praise. These are not just idle words –

they are our life. Speaking or singing these words out loud has a powerful effect on us and our situation.

Darlene Zschech says in her book Worship Changes Everything – "David tells us that God's Word is a lamp for our feet and a light for our path. Nowhere and at no time is that more important than the rocky, rugged, tangled terrain of the wilderness. We need illumination to keep us from tumbling down a ravine; we need a bright light to ward off wild animals that would attack us in the dark; we need a map to keep us from wandering in circles like the Israelites after leaving Egypt for the Promised Land. By speaking God's words in the wilderness we find deliverance."

"In the wilderness, it is a discipline to keep from continuously talking about the problem. But if we do, we keep wandering in circles long after we should have stepped into victory. Even if the feelings aren't there, we can still acknowledge God's presence with praise and thanksgiving. By God's grace, we are still to worship!"

Worshipping in the wilderness might be the last thing we feel like doing. However, when we worship, we are speaking out words in faith. These are called speech acts. These are words or utterances which have an action or consequence. They go beyond simply communicating an exchange of information. When we speak these words, we are actually doing something with them. This changes a situation.

The First Week of Lent

Tuesday

'Forget the former things; do not dwell on the past. See, I am doing a new thing! Now it springs up; do you not perceive it? I am making a way in the wilderness and streams in the wasteland' (Isaiah 43:18-19).

These words would have been familiar to Jesus. What might they have meant to him as he journeyed into the wilderness?

Meditate on these Isaiah verses today. What do you learn from them as you undertake your Lent journey?

Habakkuk 3:17-18 says:

"Though the fig-tree does not bud and there are no grapes on the vines, though the olive crop fails and the fields produce no food, though there are no sheep in the pen and no cattle in the stalls, yet I will rejoice in the Lord, I will be joyful in God my Saviour."

Worshipping God is related to thanksgiving and aligning our thoughts and words with his. Romans 10:17 tell us that, "Faith comes by hearing and hearing by the Word of God." When we speak out words of faith and simultaneously hear ourselves speaking out these words, they reinforce our trust both in God and in his goodness.

Pray

Father of my soul,

Mother of my heart,

I know your love for me is limitless beyond imagining.

You care for me as a loving parent.

Through my smallest Lenten sacrifices, help me to become less selfish and more aware of your ways.

Fan the flame of my desire to draw ever closer to you.

Guide me to seek your love.

The First Week of Lent

Wednesday

Keep your eyes fixed on God

When the Israelites wandered through the wilderness, Exodus 13:21-22 tells us that:

"By day the Lord went ahead of them in a pillar of cloud to guide them on their way and by night in a pillar of fire to give them light, so that they could travel by day or night. Neither the pillar of cloud by day nor the pillar of fire by night left its place in front of the people."

Exodus 14:19-20 also says:

'Then the angel of God, who had been travelling in front of Israel's army, withdrew and went behind them. The pillar of cloud also moved from in front and stood behind them, coming between the armies of Egypt and Israel. Throughout the night the cloud brought darkness to the one side and light to the other side; so neither went near the other all night long.'

The pillar of cloud by day and fire by night was a demonstration that God was protecting his people and was continually involved in their deliverance.

Corrie Ten Boom said: "If you look at the world, you'll be distressed. If you look within, you'll be depressed. If you look at God, you'll be at rest."

When we take our eyes off God – our pillar of cloud by day and fire by night – we end up being unable to see where we are going. We wander about in the darkness and get lost. We forget that God is nearby and ahead of us, leading us through the desert. This is what the Israelites did at numerous points throughout their journey. Keeping our eyes fixed on Jesus helps us to trust in him through difficult times.

If you gave God an hour of your day, where might the Spirit take you? Go on a prayer walk around your local community today, but don't plan your route in advance. See where the Holy Spirit prompts you to go, and pray for each street you walk down. You could invite a few friends to go on their own prayer walks, then compare thoughts afterwards to see where God led you all.

Pray

Dear Lord, you know what is in my heart. Let me be inspired by your words and by the actions of your son, Jesus. Guide me to make sacrifices this Lent in the spirit of self-denial and with greater attention to you and to those around me.

Help me to believe that you will grant me this because of the sacrifice Jesus made for me.

The First Week of Lent

Thursday

Luke tells us that Jesus was 'full of the Spirit' and 'led by the Spirit' (Luke 4:1). It's difficult to be filled or led when we're rushing around. As we come to the end of reflecting on 'setting out', let's open a space in our lives, sit still and welcome the refreshing, renewing Spirit of God.

Spend a few minutes in silence, holding an empty cup in your hands.

Each time your mind wanders, bring it back by focusing on that empty vessel ready to be filled. Think about the fruit of the spirit filling up your life.

Galatians 5:22-23

22 But the fruit of the Spirit is love, joy, peace, forbearance, kindness, goodness, faithfulness, 23 gentleness and self-control. Against such things there is no law.

Pray

Lord, I'm not always eager to do your will. I'd often much rather do my own will. Please be with me on this Lenten journey and help me to remember that your own spirit can guide me in the right direction.

I want to fix my weaknesses but the task seems overwhelming. I know that with your help, anything can be done.

With a grateful heart, I acknowledge your love and know that without you, I can do nothing.

Repentance During Lent

The First Week of Lent

Friday

Letting Go

'Now Jesus, full of the Holy Spirit, left the Jordan and was led by the Spirit into the wild. For forty wilderness days and nights he was tested by the Devil' Luke 4:1-2.

The wilderness may well be the place where we come face to face with all that is most destructive to us, but it's also the place where the Spirit can purify and refine us.

Reading the bible each day helps to bring peace and give perspective to our lives. There is no need for this to become a marathon of reading Genesis to Revelation. Instead, we can follow the gentle and prayerful practice of reading a passage from the Bible each day without any attempt to study it, but rather letting it touch us in our heart and mind. We should pause to repeat any word or phrase that strikes us and allow it to stay with us. This way of reading the Bible – Lectio Divina – goes back to early Christianity, and allows the Bible to become one of God's many ways of being with us, in the questions and doubts and struggles we have, but also in the still, small voice we need to hear.

Pray

Creator of my Life, renew me; bring me to new life in you.

Touch me and make me feel whole again.

Help me to see your love in the passion, death and resurrection of your son.

Help me to observe Lent in a way that allows me to celebrate that love.

Prepare me for these weeks of Lent, as I feel both deep sorrow for my sins and your undying love for me.

The First Week of Lent

Saturday

Jesus was tempted. Jesus, who preached and healed and was raised from the dead, was as human as we are, and he was tempted to do things that would put up barriers between him and God.

Is there something in your life which you've chosen but which has become a barrier between you and God? In your journal, write a letter to God, who loves you so much, telling God how you feel and asking for help to find your way back.

Pray

Loving God, sometimes my heart turns in every direction except towards you.

Please help me to turn my heart toward you, to gaze upon you in trust and to seek your kingdom with all of my heart. Please show me the barriers that are between us and give me the courage and strength to pull down those barriers.

Soften my hardened heart so that I might love others as a way to glorify and worship you.

Grant me this with the ever-present guidance of your spirit.

Second Sunday of Lent

The Second Week of Lent

Sunday

Addiction can be described as being in the grip of a habit that's stronger than you are, and those who live with addictions often feel oppressed by darkness and hopelessness.

For your prayerful reading this week, look up some information about local addiction services and read it through slowly, stopping to pray whenever the Spirit prompts you to.

Pray

Loving God, I pray for those who are addicted to things that harm them.

Let them find help and relief.

Bring me to your truth and help me to respond to your generous love.

Let me recognise the fullness of your love which will fill my life.

Give me the motivation and grace to reach out to others that need help.

The Second Week of Lent

Monday

Is there something in your life which feels like it's stronger than you are – maybe a fear, an addiction, a coping mechanism or a feeling of hopelessness? So often we end up shut away in shame, but we all have our struggles and we don't have to face them alone. There's great power in talking and praying together.

Connect with someone you trust this week by telling them what you're struggling with. Ask them to pray for you regularly, and agree to pray for them too.

Pray

Lord, your commandment of love is so simple and so challenging.

There is so much darkness in my life that I hide from you.

Take my hand and lead me out of the shadows of my fear.

Help me to change my heart.

Free me from the darkness in my heart.

Help me to let go of my pride, to be humble in my penance.

I want only to live the way you ask me to love, to love the way you ask me to live.

I ask this through your son, Jesus, who stands at my side today and always.

The Second Week of Lent

Tuesday

Jesus was tempted by the Devil, but some of the testing came with the circumstances. There were no creature comforts, no reassuring company, none of the familiar pastimes – nothing to make the desert more bearable. We only know how much we depend on things and people when they're not there.

What are you depending on too much? Find a way to fast from it today – or maybe for the coming week. Take time to stop and pray, asking God to help you develop new, healthier habits.

Pray

God in heaven and in my life, guide me and protect me.

Show me what I am depending on too much. Help me develop and mature so as to pull away from this dependence and depend more on You.

I so often believe I can save myself and I always end in failure.

Lead me with your love away from harm and guide me on the right path.

Show me what is in my life that is blocking You out. Loving God, show me how to develop healthier habits.

May your Spirit inspire me and make me an instrument of your love.

Thank you for your care for me.

During this season of Lent shine a light on all the areas of my life that need to develop and change.

The Second Week of Lent

Wednesday

If you know someone who's battling addiction, you may have found it difficult to know how to pray for them, especially if the battle has been a long, drawn-out one. That's where silence can be very helpful.

Spend time today sitting still in silence, holding that person in your mind. Don't try and form a prayer or think of a solution; just picture their face and imagine you're sitting together at Jesus' feet.

If you have any worries or fears, sit still, and imagine you're sitting together at Jesus' feet. Tell Jesus about it.

Pray

Please Lord, be with *******. You know their situation. Please help them. Please show me how I may be part of your plan for them.

God of Love, through this Lenten journey, purify me. Give me the desire to serve you. Free me from any temptations to judge others, to place myself above others. Please let me surrender even my impatience with others, that with your love and your grace, I might be less and less absorbed with myself, and more and more full of the desire to follow you.

Encountering the Darkness

The spiritual life always involves an encounter with darkness. The people of Israel are led through the desert into the Promised Land. Jesus began his ministry being driven into the wilderness. The garden of the resurrection is entered through his suffering on Calvary. Similarly, our faith must pass through periods of barren difficulty, doubt and despair.

But doubt is not the opposite of faith. The opposite of doubt is certainty. Doubting is part of believing. It is the shadow that is created by the light. This is why when people become Christians, we do not ask them to say that they know beyond doubt that Jesus is the one they must follow. We ask them if they believe and trust.

When we follow Christ, we are not giving our assent to a set of abstract propositions, but to a person. To the living God who is made known to us as Father, Son and Holy Spirit. We are saying that God is community, and that we are called to live our lives in community with God and with each other.

It is often in prayer that we become most aware of the dark and difficult times of the Christian journey.

Sometimes this is because we are facing a crisis or a tragedy in our life or in the life of the world. Sometimes it can be what feels like a loss of faith. We feel angry and resentful towards God. It feels as if God has let us down, or even abandoned us. Prayer suddenly feels impossible or useless. God seems absent.

When this happens prayer becomes empty, familiar words and rituals lose their comfort. Church becomes boring. Other Christians become irritating, and faith can suddenly feel a ridiculous charade. The energy of our faith is sapped.

Although these experiences are dark and terrible, they are also normal and inevitable. All the great spiritual writers speak of the desert experience as part of the Christian journey.

Many Christians are ill-prepared for the dark times that will inevitably come. Often people not only give up on prayer, but give up on God when they find themselves in the desert.

You might be feeling great despair and darkness right now. Prayer might have become very difficult. But if all you do is hold on to your desire to pray, then you are already on the road to recovery.

The Second Week of Lent

Thursday

Another word we use for temptations and dependencies is 'idols'. Idols are things which have come to have too much power and authority in our lives. When we demote them, we find real freedom.

Find three or four stones to represent 'idols' in your life which you want to topple. Walk to a quiet place, carrying them with you. Notice how heavy they feel. When you get there, lay each one on the ground as a sign of your desire to be free. Then walk home without them and enjoy the feeling of lightness.

Prayer List

Lent Reflections

Pray

Loving God, show me the idols in my life that block me from being close to you and complete in my own life. I name these idols now to you. Please grant me the knowledge and strength to be released and free.

Loving God, I hear your invitation, "Come back to me" and I am filled with such a longing to return to you.

Show me the way to return. Lead me this day in good works and send your Spirit to guide me and strengthen my faith.

I ask only to feel your love in my life today.

The Second Week of Lent

Friday

Don't make the thing you lack into an idol

When our prayers go unanswered and God doesn't seem to grant the very thing we want, it's easy to become completely focused on this thing to the point of obsession. In his book Counterfeit Gods, Tim Keller defines an idol as – "… something we cannot live without… It is anything more important to you than God, anything that absorbs your heart and imagination more than God, anything you seek to give you what only God can give. A counterfeit god is anything so central and essential to your life that, should you lose it, your life would feel hardly worth living."

In Exodus 17 or Numbers 11:4-6, the Israelites began to hunger after other kinds of food to the point they were obsessed with it. They were even willing to sacrifice their freedom in order to return to Egypt to eat anything but the manna which God provided for them every day. They allowed their desire for something other than God himself to cloud their judgment and to become all-consuming that they couldn't live without it. In effect, they had made this into an idol. This culminated in the Israelites asking Aaron in Exodus 32 to fashion them a physical idol. This took the form of a golden calf which they began to worship and to declare that this had brought them out of Egypt.

God is the only one who can meet our deepest need. Don't allow your identity to be based on the thing you lack. Tim Keller adds – "If we look to some created thing to give us the meaning, hope, and happiness that only God himself can give, it will eventually fail to deliver and break our hearts."

We may feel that our work or our relationships define us. However, it is Christ in whom we find our identity.

'Now the Lord is the Spirit, and where the Spirit of the Lord is, there is freedom.' (2 Corinthians 3:17)

Spend some time today meditating on this verse.

Pray

Loving God, I pray for freedom. I name all the idols and things that block me from you and take away my freedom.

Loving God, caring parent, I am a child who so often turns my back on your love.

Please accept my small acts of sorrow today and help to release me from the self-absorption that closes my heart to you.

As I journey through Lent, let me remember the feast you have prepared for me and let me be filled with thanks to you.

The Second Week of Lent

Saturday

Doing Without

'He ate nothing during those days, and at the end of them he was hungry. The devil said to him, "If you are the Son of God, tell this stone to become bread." Jesus answered, "It is written: 'Man shall not live on bread alone.'"" (Luke 4:2-4)

God is our provider. We get a taste of that truth in the times of plenty, when every need is met with abundance and every prayer is answered. But it's in our walk in the wilderness that we truly learn God is enough.

Pray

Loving God, you know of my struggle in the wilderness.

Please grant me wisdom and insight to understand why it had to be so.

Please walk along side with me as I walk through this wilderness.

Let me know your presence.

Grant me faith and courage.

God of infinite love, you shower me with limitless gifts in my life.

In my every thought and action today guide me to the bright and loving light of your kingdom.

Help me to be aware of the many ways you allow me to share in your life so intimately today.

Thank you for the gifts you have placed in my life.

Let me be grateful every moment of this day.

Please, Lord bless and protect me.

Amen

Third Sunday of Lent

The Third Week of Lent

Sunday

To walk in the wilderness is to be willing to have our lives stripped back; to go without; to slow down; to empty ourselves in order that God might work in us. Sometimes circumstances do the stripping back for us and sometimes we do it ourselves by choosing disciplines like simplicity.

'Desert spirituality is characterised by the pursuit of abundant simplicity – simplicity grounded in the possession of little – and the abundance of God's presence.' (Laura Swan, The Forgotten Desert Mothers: Sayings, Lives, and Stories of Early Christian Women)

Reflect on what it means to live simply in the midst of God's abundance.

Today, choose simplicity by walking somewhere instead of driving. If you would normally walk anyway, walk a longer route and slow down, giving time for prayer and reflection as you go.

Pray

Loving Father, so many times I turn away from you and always you welcome me back.

Your mercy and love give me confidence. Thank you for the invitation to share, fast and pray so that you can form a new heart within me.

Help me to strip back my life and find simplicity. Help me to empty myself so that I can be filled with you. Amen

Spend ten minutes in silence, holding an empty cup in your hands.

Each time your mind wanders, bring it back by focusing on that empty vessel ready to be filled by God.

Think about how much the cup can hold.

Hold the cup out before you.

Ask God to fill you with his love and compassion.

The Third Week of Lent

Monday

Having left behind every other human comfort, Jesus chose to fast for 40 days. It was a bold choice – even a life-threatening one – and it left him utterly dependent on God in every way. In a pale imitation of Jesus, we fast as a sign of our desire to rely on God more than we rely on food and physical comforts.

If you're able to fast safely, fast from one meal today, spending the time in prayer. You could also work out the cost of your meals and give the money to a charity working with those in food poverty.

Pray

Merciful God, please reveal yourself to me through any sacrifices I make this Lent. Show me how to change so that I might grow closer to you. Show me what work you would have me do. Show me who I should pray for. Show me how to use my time and gifts for your glory. I need your guidance, Lord, for I cannot do this alone.

Giving & Receiving

Prayer Requests

The Third Week of Lent

Tuesday

Hunger may be an uncomfortable experience for us when we fast, but for some people it is an unavoidable daily reality. Lent is a time when churches often work together to raise money for those living in poverty.

Find out what fundraising is happening in your area and connect with it this week, either by contributing financially or attending an event. Whatever you do, make sure prayer is part of your response.

Pray

God of infinite love, I thank you for Lent as it reminds me of your love and your call that I be more patient, gentle and compassionate with others. I pray for all those adults and children who are hungry today. Please show me how I can help them.

Here in the middle of Lent, I turn to you to beg for your help. Please soften my heart. Help me to let go of judging others. I ask you this, in Jesus' name.

The Third Week of Lent

Wednesday

In a relatively wealthy society, our first experience of 'lack' often comes when our prayers aren't answered in the way we'd like. The pain of unanswered prayer is a deep hunger and a true wilderness experience.

Take time today to journal about some of the prayers you still haven't seen answered in the way you'd hoped, writing honestly about your feelings and your questions. Then pause and listen to what God wants to say to you. You may still not get the answer, but more than anything, God wants you to know you're not alone.

Pray

Dear God, I sit in silence before you. Please calm my racing thoughts. I lift before you all my unanswered prayers. Show me your will. Help me to understand.

God, you love me as your own child. May I bend my life and will toward you so that I might accept your teaching and guidance.

I am so grateful for your support in my life, now and in the eternal life you are preparing for me. I beg for your help and Spirit in my life today.

The Third Week of Lent

Thursday

Jesus had grown up in a relatively busy, prosperous town in Galilee. In contrast, the desert must have been an eerily silent place to be for so long. There was no comforting buzz of activity to anaesthetise him against the pain of loss and grief. There was just the space to feel.

We're very good at anaesthetising our pain with noise and activity. Read over your Lent journal entries, then sit in silence for half an hour, letting the feelings come. Remember, you're not alone.

Pray

Loving God, show me how I anaesthetise myself from the pain and sadness in my life, be it through food, alcohol, poor relationship choices or other stuff. Let me recognise them now and name them out loud.

Loving God, please give me the strength to be released from the control of these things. I do want to change. I do want to change. I do want to change.

Loving God, thank you for your grace and love for me. Help me to find my way through the challenges in my life and have peace.

Loving God, I hear your invitation, "Come back to me" and I am filled with such a longing to return to you. Show me the way to return. Lead me this day in good works that I do in your name and send your Spirit to guide me and strengthen my faith. I ask only to feel your love in my life today.

Loving God please strengthen my faith. Let your hope and love fill me and shine out to others.

The Third Week of Lent

Friday

'There are, no doubt, passages in the New Testament which may seem at first sight to promise an invariable granting of our prayers. But that cannot be what they really mean. For in the very heart of the story we meet a glaring instance to the contrary. In Gethsemane the holiest of all petitioners prayed three times that a certain cup might pass from him. It did not. After that the idea that prayer is recommended to us as a sort of infallible gimmick may be dismissed.' (C.S. Lewis, A Grief Observed)

Read this quote through prayerfully, noticing which words or ideas the Spirit draws your attention to.

Pray

Gracious God, what do you want me to learn about prayer? Teach me how to pray.

Loving God, help me to understand. God of Mercy, I feel my heart overflowing with your tenderness. I sense your loving touch deep within my soul. I ask for your help in my weakness that I might be a true servant. I am so grateful for your love and forgiveness. Thank you for all that you have given to me. Help me be the person you want me to be.

Repentance During Lent

Tell God What's Troubling You

Finding Refreshment in the Desert

When you journey through the desert, what you look for is an oasis – a place where you can quench your thirst. The oasis will be different for each of us – it might be a familiar prayer; a verse from scripture; a piece of music; a photograph; or even some symbolic action.

Discern what it is – no matter how small and seemingly insignificant – that still connects you to God, and hold onto it tightly through the desert.

Discern what it is that still connects you to God, and hold onto it tightly.

Some of the things you have read about here can be your oasis in this desert. Even if it is just crying out the name of Jesus from the depths of sadness and fear, then you are a person of prayer, in community with God and held by Jesus. As you hold onto him and cry out to him, he is holding you.

In the Bible, the desert is always a place of discovery. The prophet Isaiah says, "The wilderness and the dry land shall be glad, the desert shall rejoice and blossom." (Isaiah 35.1)

May this be true for you, too.

"If I say, 'Surely the darkness shall cover me, and the light around me become night', even the darkness is not dark to you; the night is as bright as the day, for darkness is as light to you."

Psalm 139.11–12

Next time you are low, read Psalm 23, "The Lord is my Shepherd", which is itself a beautiful prayer.

Ask God to give you peace.

Learn off by heart a prayer that will stay with you even (maybe especially) when you feel far from God.

Thank You God

Prayers For Forgiveness

The Third Week of Lent

Saturday

Keep Drinking the Living Water

In the same way that you would need to keep drinking in a physical desert, it's important to keep yourself spiritually hydrated when you're going through a wilderness period.

Exodus 17:1-7 describes the incident where the Israelites were in the desert and became thirsty. They began to grumble against Moses, questioning why he brought them out into the desert to die of thirst.

Verses 5-6 recount God's response:

The Lord answered Moses, "Go out in front of the people. Take with you some of the elders of Israel and take in your hand the staff with which you struck the Nile, and go. I will stand there before you by the rock at Horeb. Strike the rock, and water will come out of it for the people to drink."

1 Corinthians 10:3-4 provides context for us and tells us that this rock was actually Jesus.

"They all ate the same spiritual food and drank the same spiritual drink; for they drank from the spiritual rock that accompanied them, and that rock was Christ."

There is a very real temptation in times of wilderness to search for and drink from a different well in order to try to quench our thirst. We can seek after many other things with which to fill ourselves. For example, if we lack relationships, we can try to fill that need for intimacy with other things in the hope that it will satisfy our loneliness or longing. We can also make these other things into idols.

We can fool ourselves into thinking that these other wells are the ones we are actually thirsty for. That they will quench our thirst if only we could drink from them. But we remain thirsty even after we've had a drink, and it does not satisfy.

"Everyone who drinks this water will be thirsty again, but whoever drinks the water I give them will never thirst. Indeed, the water I give them will become in them a spring of water welling up to eternal life." John 4:13-14

'I'd never forget you – never. Look, I've written your names on the backs of my hands. The walls you're rebuilding are never out of my sight.'

(Isaiah 49:16 The Message)

Meditate on God's love for you, giving thanks to the one who will always be with you and who will always be enough.

Pray

Loving God, I hear your invitation, "Come back to me" and I am filled with such a longing to return to you.

Show me the way to return.

Lead me this day in good works that I do in your name and send your Spirit to guide me and strengthen my faith.

I ask only to feel your love in my life today.

Loving God, help me to find my way out of the wilderness and walk back to you, stronger, refreshed, ready to do your will and walk your walk.

God of Mercy and Understanding, I know that with help I can open my heart more fully to the mysteries of the suffering and death of your son.

Help me to be humble in this journey and remember that any mercy and compassion I feel is a gift from you.

I await the joy of Easter with new longing and patience.

Fourth Week of Lent

Sunday

There is a whisper of spring in the air. The nights have more light. Give praise and thanks.

Losing Control

'The devil led him up to a high place and showed him in an instant all the kingdoms of the world. And he said to him, "I will give you all their authority and splendour; it has been given to me, and I can give it to anyone I want to. If you worship me, it will all be yours." Jesus answered, "It is written: 'Worship the Lord your God and serve him only.'" (Luke 4:5-8)

Jesus has all power and authority, but he didn't get there by claiming his right to it. He got there through surrender and submission, through pouring himself out and losing control, even unto death.

Pray

Gracious God, please give me the wisdom and courage to hand control over to you, no matter how difficult or tormented are my circumstances.

Loving Creator of mine, teach me to follow the example of your Son, to be worthy of being called one his people: a Christian. Help me to live each day as he did, turning hatred to love and conflict to peace. I await the new life with eagerness, faith and a deep gratitude.

O Lord, support me all the day long through the challenges of this life, until the shadows lengthen, and the evening comes, and the busy world is hushed, and the fever of life is over, and the work is done.

Then, Lord, in thy mercy grant me a safe lodging, a holy rest, and peace at the last; through Jesus Christ our Lord.

Amen.

(John Henry Newman)

The Fourth Week of Lent

Monday

Power and authority are tempting because being in control feels safe, whereas being out of control and thrown into chaos can feel frightening. Sometimes we find real safety and peace when our self-constructed security has to be destroyed. Crisis brings change that can bring a new way of living and healing.

At this time our control and securities are being shaken. This should not undermine our faith in God, but it can be a means of helping us to rediscover our real safety, which nothing can destroy, not even death itself. True safety through faith in God enables us to live at peace in insecurity, offers us certainty in uncertainty and comfort in confusion. In this situation of personal chaos, with the grace of God, we can smile through the tears.

Connect today with someone who's in a situation where they feel completely out of control. Ask how you can pray for them. Assure them of your love and care.

Pray

Gracious God, guide me through my wilderness. Let this time strengthen my faith and rediscover my relationship with you. Let me learn to live in peace even during times of uncertainty and let me find comfort when there is confusion. In my situation of personal chaos let me find rest.

Dear God, help me to reach out to others that are going through personal chaos.

I name those people by calling out loud to you.

Show me what I may do to ease their situation and let them see your love.

God who created me, you offer me new life through your Son. While I see new life all around me, I don't always recognise the new life you offer me. Help me to grow this Lent in an awareness of the gifts you place in my life and in a greater appreciation for your care. Give me the courage to ask for help.

The Fourth Week of Lent

Tuesday

Are you facing a situation where you feel powerless and out of control? Maybe it even feels like your world is crumbling around your feet. Jesus' response to that feeling was simply to worship. Sit a while in silence today, acknowledging your weakness and your inability to change what needs changing, but declaring from the depths of your soul that Jesus is King of kings and Lord of lords.

Pray

Loving God, I ask you to help me prepare to understand and embrace the challenges in my life.

I don't always see the beauty and mystery of this season of Lent and often I run from the pain.

Help me to see how your saving grace and your loving touch in my life can fill me with joyful praise of the salvation you have gifted to me.

Prayer List

Prayers Answered

The Fourth Week of Lent

Wednesday

Jesus lived in a society where some had great power and others had no power at all. Does this remind you of the world we live in today? Some people have the world at their feet while others sleep on the pavement.

Go on a 'prayer walk' today, planning your route to pass the places of power in your community (council offices, law courts, prosperous businesses etc) as well as the places of deprivation and powerlessness. Tell God what your feelings are and ask him how he can use you to bring Glory to His Name.

Pray

Loving and merciful God, help me to process the power structure of the world I live in. Show me your will and how I can carry it out. What am I to do to improve and make better this world I live in?

I am so aware of my sins and weaknesses, but as painfully aware of my faults as I am, let me also remember your tender love, your gentle and limitless forgiveness. I come before you filled with pain and guilt but look into your eyes and see the forgiving love I so long for in my life. Help me to forgive the same way. Teach me to love as you love.

The Fourth Week of Lent

Thursday

John the Baptist knew what it was to live in a wilderness and to submit to God. Here's what he said about Jesus: 'Therefore, I am filled with joy at his success. He must become greater and greater, and I must become less and less' (John 3:29-30).

Meditate on these words today. What does it mean for Jesus to become greater and for us to become less?

Pray

Merciful and Loving God, I know that the tiny sacrifices I make this Lent can never serve as a real penance in my life. Help me to make my whole life one of following your Son. Fill me with your love. Let your love shine out from within me and guide my life in this sacred journey toward the Easter joy you offer me.

The Fourth Week of Lent

Friday

Power, authority and control are seductive. Perhaps it's no surprise, then, that one of Jesus' temptations was the offer of being put in charge of everything straight away. Yet he chose the humbler, harder way.

Is there a situation where you know you cling on to power or control?

What could you do to fast from doing that today? Could you stay silent, delegate something or let someone else choose?

Pray

Loving God of forgiveness, I come before you humbled and sad in the face of my own repeated failings. I hold out my hands to you, asking for mercy. It is then that I feel you reach out and take my hands in your loving grasp. Thank you for the love you pour out on me so lavishly.

Help me to follow more closely in the path you have set for me, the path of your Son.

Let me call to mind the fractured relationships and injustices of this world that grieve the heart of God. Let me remember my part in this and show me a path to redemption.

God of heaven and earth, as Jesus taught his disciples to be persistent in prayer, give me patience and courage never to lose hope, but always to bring my prayers before you; through my Saviour Jesus Christ. Amen.

Praise God

Reflections

The Fourth Week of Lent

Saturday

Leaders come in all shapes and sizes, and we admire some more than others. Think of a famous person (living or dead) whose leadership you admire. Think about the circumstances they faced and the choices they made. How do they compare with the qualities of leadership shown by Jesus? What do you hear God saying to you about this?

How do I pray when prayer seems impossible?

Throughout Christian history, when people sought to deepen their relationship with God they went into the desert. They pursued isolation. This way of living the Christian vocation was called the solitary life.

Abba Moses, one of the Desert Fathers, used to say to his novices, "Go to your cell, and your cell will teach you everything."

Those early monks who fled into the desert were imitating Jesus in his isolation. There are many times in the gospels where Jesus deliberately removes himself from people. He disappears off to a deserted place to pray (Mark 1.32). He dismisses the crowds and goes up a mountain on his own (Matthew 14.23). He sits by a well in the desert (John 4.5). He prays on his own on the night before his death (Luke 22.41). In particular, the monks remembered the days Jesus spent in the wilderness and the temptations he faced there (Matthew 4.1–11).

Pray

My loving Lord, it's so hard to live in the world sometimes and to love it the way Jesus did seems impossible. Help me to be inspired by his love and guided by his example.

Most of all, I want to accept that I can't do it alone, and that trying is an arrogance of self-centeredness.

I need you, dear God, to give me support in this journey.

Show me how to unlock my heart so that I am less selfish. Let me be less fearful of the pain and darkness that will be transformed by you into Easter joy.

The Fifth Week of Lent

Sunday

Losing Face

'The devil led him to Jerusalem and had him stand on the highest point of the temple. "If you are the Son of God," he said, "throw yourself down from here. For it is written: 'He will command his angels concerning you to guard you carefully; they will lift you up in their hands, so that you will not strike your foot against a stone.'" Jesus answered, "It is said: 'Do not put the Lord your God to the test.'"' (Luke 4:9-12)

A dramatic high-dive followed by an angelic rescue would have been a short-cut to fame and acclaim for Jesus, but the wilderness is where we dare to say 'no' to human notions of success.

In the seclusion of the desert, the Devil showed Jesus Jerusalem – that bustling city where a budding rabbi might make his name. If Jesus was doubting himself, that kind of popularity must have seemed tempting.

You are enough. Whatever you've achieved in life; whatever others think of you; whatever you think of yourself – know today that God says you are enough. Spend some time in silence, letting that truth sink in.

Pray

Lord, what you ask of my life seems so right. It is how I want to live, following your Son, Jesus, so closely. Yet I fail so often to stay on that path. I cannot do it alone, loving Lord. I need your help and guidance. I need to remember your love for me and I want to remember how very much I need you in my life.

Most Loving God, thank you that you remain constant with me through all the changing scenes of life. Help me to trust you in times of joy and in sorrow. Be my shepherd in the darkness and in the light, so that I might be a living beacon of hope for others.

The Fifth Week of Lent

Monday

'Be there for me, God, for I keep trusting in you. Don't allow my foes to gloat over me or the shame of defeat to overtake me. For how could anyone be disgraced when he has entwined his heart with you?' (Psalm 25:2-3 The Passion Translation)

Meditate on these words today. They help remind us what really matters and where our security really lies.

Pray

God of love, I know that you are the source of all that is good in my life. Help me to remember that You are always there for me. No matter what storms are raging around me, give me the faith and trust to know that I can depend and lean on You. Help me to move from the life of sin to which I so often cling, into the new life of grace you offer me. You know what I need to prepare for your kingdom. Bless me with those gifts. During this Lent help me to reflect on your love for me and how that love can transform me and draw me closer to you.

I am Grateful For

I Give You My Time, Treasurers and Talents

The Fifth Week of Lent

Tuesday

If Jesus had jumped from the top of the Temple in the middle of Jerusalem, some people would have been impressed. It's tempting to want to do something just because you know it will impress people. If you're honest, are there things you know you do only because you want to impress others? Could you fast from those things today?

Pray

Loving God, help me to live for you and what you think of me and not for what others think about me. Forgive me if I have been shallow and vain. You know me so well. You know how many hairs are on my head. You have heard my complaints, my impatience. Sometimes I become frightened when I move away from you. Guide my heart back to you. Help me to think beyond my own wants and to desire only to do your will. Thank you for the many blessings in my life and for the ways I feel your presence.

The Fifth Week of Lent

Wednesday

Our default self is selfish, just thinking about our own needs and time. When a situation arises try to put personal needs to one side and view the picture as God would and what would He do to make it better. When Jesus was asked the question, "what is the greatest commandment?" he didn't say: "Be Yourself." He said: "Love God and love your neighbour." The Christian wisdom is, that paradoxically, we find our true self when we lose it, by being turned, not inwards in self-obsession, but outwards in love for the God who made us and our neighbours who need us.

Pray

Loving Creator, let me never test you. Let me be a good and faithful servant. I know in your great love for me, you see the deep sorrow in my heart. Hear my prayers which are offered with trust in you. Be with me in both mind and heart as I renew my life in your spirit.

Persevere in Prayer

Self Examination During Lent

A Pathway to Prayer

Examen – Pray over the day

It is suggested this prayer is done at the end of every day, but some people find first thing in the morning is more helpful. This prayer is a reflection to become more aware of God at work in your life. It should also throw up negative experiences which you may be able to avoid in the future.

Be still, remember the God who loves you is present with you now.

Look back over the day.

Ask God to shine a light into your heart so that looking back you may be able to see God at work.

Pay attention to your emotions.

What brought you joy?

Is there anything you feel unhappy about?

Talk to God about your day.

For what do you feel most thankful? Give thanks.

For what do you feel least thankful? Hand this over to God.

What have you learned from the day, how have you grown?

Look forward to tomorrow.

How might you make the best of the day.

1. Ask God for light. I want to look at my day with God's eyes, not my own.

2. Give thanks. The day I have just lived is a gift from God. Be grateful for it.

3. Review the day. Carefully look back on the day just completed, being guided by the Holy Spirit.

4. Face your shortcomings. Face up to what is wrong in my life and in me.

5. Look toward the day to come. I ask where I need God in the day to come.

Real prayer is about change, and change is never easy.

Why did Jesus spend so much time in prayer?

Maybe, like us, he needed to spend time in prayer and reflection in order to know God his loving Father better and to find out what God wanted.

Even the relationship between Jesus and the Father needed communication in order to grow.

The Fifth Week of Lent

Thursday

We tend to fear failure. Perhaps that's why it's so tempting to conform to society's view of what success should look like. Spend some time journaling about failure. What do you consider to be your greatest failures? How did they happen? What do you wish you had done differently? What do you think God would say about them? Now look at an example in your life of a time you thought was a failure but afterwards it turned into a blessing.

Pray

Lord, as I look over the failures in my life, I am sad. Please reveal to me how I can turn my failures into glory for you. What lessons should I learn? All I want is to be faithful to you in my life, but so often I fail. Free me from my many sins that block me in my relationship with you. Guide me to the life I will share with you. I praise and thank you for all your love for me and the many great blessings you have bestowed on me.

Loving God, you know of my struggle in the wilderness. Please grant me wisdom and insight to understand why it had to be so. Loving Father, so many times I turn away from you and always you welcome me back. Your mercy and love give me confidence. Thank you for the invitation to share, fast and pray so that you can form a new heart within me. Help me to strip back my life and find simplicity. Help me to empty myself so that I can be filled with you.

The Fifth Week of Lent

Friday

The Devil took Jesus to two high places, a mountain and the Temple roof; but Jesus knew his route was downwards: down from glory, through humanity, even to death on a cross (Philippians 2:5-8).

Go on a walk today, starting in a high place (the top of a hill, for instance) and walking downwards. As you walk, reflect on what it means to refuse the temptations of the high places – popularity, wealth and worldly success – and to choose the humbling way of Christ.

Pray

Most forgiving Lord, again and again you welcome me back into your loving arms. Grant me freedom from the heavy burdens of guilt and unhappiness that weigh me down and keep me so far from you. Give me the courage and wisdom to turn away from those things that I think bring me happiness but, in reality, hold me down and bring me misery. I name them now to you, dear Lord.

The Fifth Week of Lent

Saturday

'Jesus returned to Galilee in the power of the Spirit, and news about him spread through the whole countryside. He was teaching in their synagogues, and everyone praised him.' (Luke 4:14-15)

In the coming days of Holy Week, we will journey with Jesus through a far deeper wilderness than the one we've just been reading about. As we track with the Easter story, look back over your wilderness wanderings and learn how these losses and how you let go enables you to live more fully in the power of the Holy Spirit. What are the lessons you have learnt this Lent?

Pray

Loving God, show me what you have taught me this Lent. Help to recognise what you are saying to me and act about it.

Loving God, Your eternal watchfulness keeps me safe from harm. Thank you for all you have revealed to me this Lent. I want to change. I want to live my life for you. I want to do your will. I am filled with a great happiness when I feel your endless love for me. Thank you for your care for me. I ask you to protect from harm those who are hungry, in fear or homeless tonight.

Holy Week

Palm Sunday

'He came in peace to give the people peace. They preferred salvation from taxation to salvation of their souls – and so in a few days they would prefer Barabbas to be freed instead of Jesus. Jesus could see that this was their mindset, and so in the midst of this praise, with people waving the palm branches like a national flag, Jesus wept.' (Paul Wallace, 'Palm Sunday')

Read and ponder these words as you celebrate Palm Sunday today.

Pray

This Palm Sunday I am thinking about the events of Holy Week. Loving God, I am just beginning to realise how much you love me. Your son, Jesus was humble and obedient. He fulfilled your will for him by becoming human and suffering. I ask you for the desire to become more humbler so that my own life might also bear witness to you. I want to use the small sufferings I have in this world to give you glory. Please, Lord, guide my mind with your truth. Strengthen my life by the example of Jesus. Help me to be with Jesus in this week as he demonstrates again his total love for me. He died so that I would no longer be separated from you. Help me to feel how close you are and to live in union with you.

Holy Week

Monday

Have faith that God is using the wilderness experience for your good.

God led the Israelites into the desert for a reason.

God chose not to lead his people directly into the Promised Land after escaping Egypt, even though he could have easily done so. At the time, it was occupied, and the Israelites would not have survived an onslaught from their enemies. They would also have still wanted to return to Egypt if they faced war. They would have lacked a true identity, unsure of whether they were truly God's people or still slaves of Egypt.

Their identity was still based on many other things rather than finding their identity in God. How easy it is to turn these things into idols, hoping they will give us the affirmation, assurance or security we seek.

God used the wilderness to forge their identity through hardship and trial and prepare them for when they did finally enter the Promised Land. He may be doing the same thing to us as we go through our own spiritual desert.

In Deuteronomy 8:2-3, Moses also provides us with another reason for going through the wilderness:

"Remember how the Lord your God led you all the way in the wilderness these forty years, to humble and test you in order to know what was in your heart, whether or not you would keep his commands. He humbled you, causing you to hunger and then feeding you with manna, which neither you nor your ancestors had known, to teach you that man does not live on bread alone but on every word that comes from the mouth of the Lord."

It was not the complaining or grumbling alone that led to the Israelites being in the desert for a longer period of time. Rather, their complaining was the outward sign of the inward state of their hearts. It revealed they were not yet fully acquainted or allied with God. They were still looking behind to where they had been before. Until their hearts were right, God would continue to use the wilderness experience to refine them and make them into the people he desired them to be.

We need to live not on bread alone but on every word that comes from God. This is a truth that Jesus recognised when he was in the wilderness himself and tempted by the devil.

Your own wilderness experience may not be pleasant, know that God has not forgotten you and is working in your life. He is using the experience for your good and to work out his purposes in you. He wants you to find your identity in him alone and to make you the person you were meant to be.

The wilderness experience depleted Jesus' resources considerably. Matthew's Gospel tells us that angels came and attended him before he returned home (Matthew 4:11).

Spend some time journaling today, writing about several moments when you've seen God's provision over the past six weeks, either in your own life or in the lives of those around you.

Pray

God of love, my prayer is simple: Your son, Jesus, suffered and died for me. I know only that I cannot have real strength unless I rely on you. I cannot feel protected from my many weaknesses until I turn to you for forgiveness and your unalterable love. Help me to share this strength, protection and love with others.

Holy Week

Tuesday

Earlier in this Lent journey, we considered what it must have been like for Jesus to choose to set out from home, leaving friends, family, work and worship rhythms, to go wherever the Spirit might lead him.

Go for a walk and a ponder today. Where has the Spirit led you over the past six weeks? What have you discovered about yourself and about God?

Preparation for prayer: Begin by stilling; then dedicating the time of prayer to God and asking God that all you think, feel and imagine are for the glory of God. Ask that God may really communicate with you in prayer.

Pray

God of such unwavering love, how do I "celebrate" the passion and death of Jesus? I often want to look the other way and not watch, not stay with Jesus in his suffering. Give me the strength to see his love with honesty and compassion and to feel deeply your forgiveness and mercy for me. Help me to understand how to "celebrate" this week. I want to be able to recognise my weaknesses and imperfections as I journey with Jesus this week.

Prayer Requests

Thank You God

Lord Help Me

Looking Back

Holy Week

Wednesday

In Christian tradition, today is the day when we remember the story of the woman who gave up her most precious possession for the sake of worship. She broke her jar of priceless nard, the heirloom which would have secured her future, and anointed Jesus with the perfume in an extravagant demonstration of her love.

Meditate on her story (Mark 14:3-9).

3 While he was in Bethany, reclining at the table in the home of Simon the Leper, a woman came with an alabaster jar of very expensive perfume, made of pure nard. She broke the jar and poured the perfume on his head.

4 Some of those present were saying indignantly to one another, "Why this waste of perfume? 5 It could have been sold for more than a year's wages and the money given to the poor." And they rebuked her harshly.

6 "Leave her alone," said Jesus. "Why are you bothering her? She has done a beautiful thing to me. 7 The poor you will always have with you, and you can help them any time you want. But you will not always have me. 8 She did what she could. She poured perfume on my body beforehand to prepare for my burial. 9 Truly I tell you, wherever the gospel is preached throughout the world, what she has done will also be told, in memory of her."

What might costly, sacrificial worship look like for Jesus' Church today? What might we need to be ready to let go, in order to love with that same joyous extravagance?

Pray

Gracious God, show me how this reading can apply to my life this Lent. Loving God, please stay with me as I struggle with the trials and challenges that life throws at me. Enhance my trust in you. Help me to be humble and accepting like your son, Jesus. I want to turn to you with the same trust he had in your love.

Lent Reflections

Repentance During Lent

Holy Week

Maundy Thursday

Maundy Thursday commemorates the Last Supper Jesus shared with his disciples.

At St James's Church Piccadilly on Maundy Thursday, the Clergy wash the feet of the people who have attended the service, in remembrance of this selfless act by Jesus.

John 13:1-17, 31b-35

13:1 Now before the festival of the Passover, Jesus knew that his hour had come to depart from this world and go to the Father. Having loved his own who were in the world, he loved them to the end. 13:2 The devil had already put it into the heart of Judas son of Simon Iscariot to betray him. And during supper 13:3 Jesus, knowing that the Father had given all things into his hands, and that he had come from God and was going to God, 13:4 got up from the table, took off his outer robe, and tied a towel around himself.

13:5 Then he poured water into a basin and began to wash the disciples' feet and to wipe them with the towel that was tied around him. 13:6 He came to Simon Peter, who said to him, "Lord, are you going to wash my feet?" 13:7 Jesus answered, "You do not know now what I am doing, but later you will understand."13:8 Peter said to him, "You will never wash my feet." Jesus answered, "Unless I wash you, you have no share with me."

13:9 Simon Peter said to him, "Lord, not my feet only but also my hands and my head!" 13:10 Jesus said to him, "One who has bathed does not need to wash, except for the feet, but is entirely clean. And you are clean, though not all of you."13:11 For he knew who was to betray him; for this reason he said, "Not all of you are clean."

13:12 After he had washed their feet, had put on his robe, and had returned to the table, he said to them, "Do you know what I have done to you? 13:13 You call me Teacher and Lord--and you are right, for that is what I am. 13:14 So if I, your Lord and Teacher, have washed your feet, you also ought to wash one another's feet.

13:15 For I have set you an example, that you also should do as I have done to you. 13:16 Very truly, I tell you, servants are not greater than their master, nor are messengers greater than the one who sent them. 13:17 If you know these things, you are blessed if you do them.

13:31b When he had gone out, Jesus said, "Now the Son of Man has been glorified, and God has been glorified in him. 13:32 If God has been glorified in him, God will also glorify him in himself and will glorify him at once.

13:33 Little children, I am with you only a little longer. You will look for me; and as I said to the Jews so now I say to you, 'Where I am going, you cannot come.'

13:34 I give you a new commandment, that you love one another. Just as I have loved you, you also should love one another. 13:35 By this everyone will know that you are my disciples, if you have love for one another."

Imagine you are at the Last Supper, listening to Jesus in a room with the Disciples.

Be still before God. Ask God that all you think, feel and imagine are for the glory of God.

Pray

Loving Provider, you gather me in this upper room with your son, to be fed by your love.

At that supper, Jesus told us to "love one another" and I know that is the heart of his gift, his sacrifice for me.

When you come close to the end of the prayer you are invited to have a conversation with Jesus. Imagine yourself talking to Jesus as a friend; a familiar conversation talking about whatever concerns you.

How does Jesus reply? God can speak through our imagination. Often, we seem to get unexpected and rapid replies.

Prayers

Lent Reflections

Holy Week

Good Friday

Good Friday is the day when we remember that Jesus relinquished all control, allowing himself to fall into death, in order that we might fall into the arms of everlasting love, forgiven, healed and renewed.

Over the centuries, Good Friday has also been a day when God's people would fast. Now, it is marked as the start of a holiday weekend, so it's easy to forget the significance of it. Can you find a way to fast from something today, to remind yourself that God's love holds you, even when you feel out of control?

On earth as in heaven we seek God's kingdom – that is God's reign of justice and peace – on earth as in heaven. We seek to align our will with the will of God. Even Jesus had to learn this in his earthly life and ministry. We see this when he battled with the devil in the wilderness. We see it most poignantly in the garden of Gethsemane when he prayed that, if it were possible, God might take the cup away from him. After much struggle and anguish, Jesus arrives at a point where he can completely accept and receive God's will for his life.

Pray

My Lord, your son has suffered so much, shed so much blood. Thank you for doing this for me.

I have so many faults, and my nature is so full of weakness, and yet your son Jesus has died on the cross for me.

I know your grace has the power to cleanse me of my many sins and to make me more like Jesus.

Let me reach a point where I can completely accept and receive your will in my life.

Thank you for your goodness and love for me.

I ask you, Father, to watch over me – always.

Holy Saturday

It's Holy Saturday, the day when all fell silent. Jesus had died and his disciples were coming to terms with having lost their teacher and their friend. Grief is always a wilderness. Spend some time in silence, holding in your heart before God all those you know who are walking the deserts of grief today.

If it helps, write down their names:

Pray

Eternal God, to whom all hearts are open, all desires known, and from whom no secrets are hidden; cleanse the thoughts of my heart by the inspiration of your Holy Spirit, that I may perfectly love you, and worthily magnify your holy name; through Christ our Lord. Amen.

I pray for those who are grieving today. Draw close to them God and give them peace.

Thank you, Lord, for desert experiences, when being confronted with myself makes me realise my need of you.

Easter Sunday

Happy Easter – Praise The Lord

Setting out, letting go, doing without, losing control, losing face…these are all a kind of death, yet they're also the way to resurrection life. Jesus came out of the wilderness in the power of the Spirit; Jesus came out of the tomb with resurrection life in his veins. As you celebrate Easter today, may you know that, through Jesus Christ, God himself has raised you from the dead and the power of the Spirit is at work in you.

Connect with others today, praying for each one by name as you wish them a Happy Easter.

Easter Prayer

When everything was dark and it seemed that the sun would never shine again, your love broke through. Your love was too strong, too wide, too deep for death to hold.

The sparks cast by your love dance and spread and burst forth with resurrection light.

Gracious God, I praise you for the light of new life made possible through Jesus. I praise you for the light of new life that shone on the first witnesses of resurrection. I praise you for the light of new life that continues to shine in hearts today.

I pray that the Easter light of life, hope and joy, will live on each day; and that I will be a bearer of that light into the lives of others.

Lord, you've guided me through the difficult days of Lent, encouraging me along the way.

I pray as I move on from Lent, that you'll guide me and remind me of my Saviour's ultimate gift and the promise of new, abundant, eternal life for all who believe and trust in him, your precious son, Jesus. Amen.

Lent Reflections

Looking Back

Prayer Requests

Prayers Answered

If you have any suggestions for this book please email
lentjournal@gmail.com

Please consider leaving a favourable review on Amazon for Lent Publications' books so that other Christians may discover them.

Thank you

May the road rise up to meet you.
May the wind be always at your back.
May the sun shine warm upon your face; the rains fall soft upon your fields and until we meet again,
May God hold you in the palm of His hand.

Printed in Great Britain
by Amazon